Basketball Superstar
Stephen Curry

by Jon M. Fishman

BUMBA BOOKS™

LERNER PUBLICATIONS ◆ MINNEAPOLIS

D1474549

Note to Educators

Throughout this book, you'll find critical-thinking questions. These can be used to engage young readers in thinking critically about the topic and in using the text and photos to do so.

Lerner Publications Company
A division of Lerner Publishing Group, Inc.
241 First Avenue North
Minneapolis, MN 55401 USA

For reading levels and more information, look up this title at www.lernerbooks.com.

Library of Congress Cataloging-in-Publication Data

Names: Fishman, Jon M., author.
Title: Basketball superstar Stephen Curry / by Jon M. Fishman.
Description: Minneapolis, Minnesota : Lerner Publications, [2019] | Series: Bumba Books—Sports Superstars | Includes bibliographical references and index. | Audience: Ages: 4–7. | Audience: Grades: K to Grade 3.
Identifiers: LCCN 2018014516 (print) | LCCN 2018017324 (ebook) | ISBN 9781541542983 (eb pdf) | ISBN 9781541538481 (library binding : alk. paper) | ISBN 9781541545762 (paperback : alk. paper)
Subjects: LCSH: Curry, Stephen, 1988—Juvenile literature. | African American basketball players—United States—Biography—Juvenile literature. | Basketball players—United States—Biography—Juvenile literature. | Golden State Warriors (Basketball team)—History—Juvenile literature.
Classification: LCC GV884.C88 (ebook) | LCC GV884.C88 F55 2019 (print) | DDC 796.323092 [B]—dc23

LC record available at https://lccn.loc.gov/2018014516

Manufactured in the United States of America
1 - 45031 - 35858 - 6/15/2018

Table of Contents

Shooting Star 4

Basketball Gear 22

Picture Glossary 23

Read More 24

Index 24

Shooting Star

Stephen Curry is a basketball champion.

His team is the Golden State Warriors.

Stephen started playing basketball as a kid.

He loved basketball.

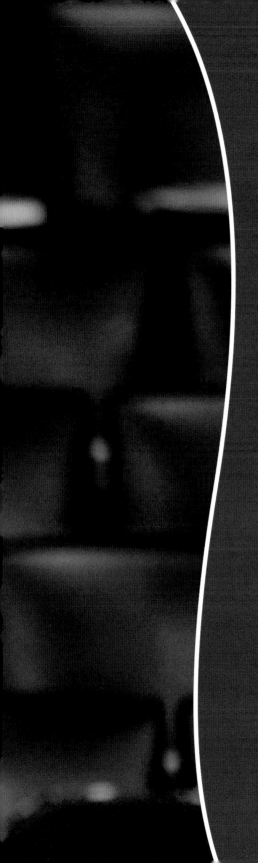

Stephen's dad played
basketball too.
He showed Stephen how
to shoot baskets.

**How do people
get better at
something?**

Stephen played basketball in college.

His team was the Davidson Wildcats.

Next, Stephen joined the

Golden State Warriors.

The team lost more games

than they won.

13

Stephen helped the team get better. In 2015, Golden State became champions.

Why do people work as a team?

Fans loved to watch Stephen play.

He scored lots of points.

Golden State became

champions again in 2017.

No team could beat them!

Stephen and his team are

just getting started.

Their future is golden!

Basketball Gear

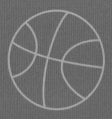

basketball

jersey

shoes

shorts

Picture Glossary

champion

winner of the top prize

college

a school after high school

fans

people who like a sport

shoot

throw toward the basket

Read More

Flynn, Brendan. *Basketball Time!* Minneapolis: Lerner Publications, 2017.

Murray, Laura K. *Stephen Curry.* Mankato, MN: Creative Education, 2017.

Nelson, Robin. *From Leather to Basketball Shoes.* Minneapolis: Lerner Publications, 2015.

Index

baskets, 9

champion, 4, 15, 19

Davidson Wildcats, 11

Golden State Warriors, 4, 12, 15, 19

points, 16

team, 4, 11–12, 15, 19–20

Photo Credits

Image credits: Amy Salveson/Independent Picture Service (basketball icons throughout); Thearon W. Henderson/Getty Images, p. 5; Streeter Lecka/Getty Images, p. 7; FREDERIC J. BROWN/AFP/Getty Images, pp. 8–9, 23 (bottom right); Chris Seward/Raleigh News & Observer/Tribune News Service/Getty Images, pp. 10, 23 (top right); Ezra Shaw/Getty Images, p. 13; Gregory Shamus/Getty Images, pp. 14–15; Stephen M. Dowell/Orlando Sentinel/Tribune News Service/Getty Images, p. 17; Ronald Martinez/Getty Images, pp. 18, 23 (top left); Jonathan Bachman/Getty Images, pp. 20–21; Billion Photos/Shutterstock.com, p. 22 (basketball); Zovteva/Shutterstock.com, p. 22 (jersey); Milos Vucicevic/Shutterstock.com, p. 22 (shoes); Mark Herreid/Shutterstock.com, p. 22 (shorts); Doug Pensinger/Getty Images, p. 23 (bottom left).

Cover: Thearon W. Henderson/Getty Images.